YOUR PASSION YOUR PURPOSE

Five Undeniable Truths To Propel You Into Your Purpose

DR. SHIRLEY PIERRE ROBERTSON

YOUR PASSION YOUR PURPOSE

Five Undeniable Truths to Propel You Into Your Purpose

By Dr Shirley Pierre Robertson
www.theoraclegroupinc.net; Published by The Oracle Group
International Publishing, Washington, DC.;
for enquires.....www.theoraclegroupinc.net

This book, or any parts thereof may not be reproduced in any form, stored in a retrieval system, or transmitted either electronically, mechanically, photocopying, recording, or otherwise without the prior written authorization from the publisher, except as provided by the United States of America copyright law. For information and enquiries, contact the publishing department at www.theoraclegroupinc.net; Published by The Oracle Group International Publishing, Washington, DC.; for enquires.....www.theoraclegroupinc.net

Unless otherwise indicated, all scriptural references were taken from the Holy Bible, New International Version (NIV).
Copyright @ 1973, 1978, 1984, by
The International Bible Society.

The New King James Version (NKJV). Copyright @ 1979, 1980, 1982 by Thomas Nelson, Inc., publishers. The publishing department at the www.theoraclegroupinc.net; Published by The Oracle Group International Publishing, Washington, DC.;
for enquires.....www.theoraclegroupinc.net

Cover design by Divine Kemayu Nana

Copyright @ 2017 by Shirley Pierre Robertson

ISBN: 978-0-9991584-0-1

DEDICATION

To the resilient and brilliant spirits of men and women who seek to find meaning in life for being and becoming their true selves.

To the fearless trailblazers who sacrificed often times with their lives, refusing to accept the status quo.

But most importantly: To Him who paid the ultimate price in order to exchange our bitter cups for His cup of freedom and restoration; He made it possible for me to return to His original plan and purpose for my life.

CONTENTS

ACKNOWLEDGMENT vii

INTRODUCTION 1

CHAPTER ONE 5

CHAPTER TWO 11

CHAPTER THREE 17

CHAPTER FOUR 27

CHAPTER FIVE 35

ABOUT THE AUTHOR 53

ACKNOWLEDGMENT

The courage to write this book grew as a result of the many years of gentle nudging and persuasion received from those who believed that I had something distinctly different to share with others. My learning and hands on experience as a Mental Health Professional, Educator, Christian Life Coach and Minister, along with my personal life experiences, prepared me to embark upon this journey of "paying it forward" or giving back aspects of that which was given to me.

To my deceased parents, Nicholson and Euphemia Pierre who believed that I was special, and had the ability to achieve beyond my wildest imagination. I thank God often for having chosen you to fulfill His plan for my birth. Your love, support, and frequent expressions of "old time terminologies" helped to prepare me to travel on this pathway called life.

DR. SHIRLEY PIERRE ROBERTSON

To my husband Allan whose love, support and frequent reminders of my several abilities kept me focused on purpose and destiny. I love you for helping me to grow and become the woman that I am today.

To my children: Richard, Michelle, Marcelle, Roger and Margo, who in your own unique way contributed to the completion of this book. I love you all dearly for this. To Divine, Windsor and Junie; my sons and daughter from other mothers, you are gems and I love you all.

To my grandchildren: Laurel, Timothy, Margeau, Pierre and Noemi, you are irreplaceable.

To the numerous individuals who intentionally and unwittingly helped to define my growth and development; I respect and thank you for your contribution to my journey.

INTRODUCTION

Undeniable Truths

Have you ever felt as if there is more to life than what you are currently experiencing? That the failed strategies utilized in the past did not satisfy the void, the emptiness, the frustration you felt as a result of not finding true meaning and significance for your life? Are you hungry for change? Then give yourself permission to move from your current place of emptiness. Realize that the time is now, if ever, for the sleeping giant that is resting dormant within you to rise up and take its rightful position on this planet. It is time to discover who you are, whose you are, and your purpose for being who the Creator says that you are. Truth be told, it is time to introduce yourself to the real you!

However, for this type of far-reaching and sweeping change to occur, the appropriate response must be one in which the determination to embrace this period as a formidable and pulsating experience is followed with visible signs of forward movement. Being willing to move from your familiar place, your place of comfort, even your place of discomfort can be challenging to say the least. Yet, the new norm cannot be business as usual because you were not created to follow the status quo.

But then, you must be aware of the fact that change is costly, it can be stressful, and a transformational energy is required to lift yourself up from your current position in order to take the first step forward and obtain your deliverance from captivity and oppression. Yet, in actuality, deliverance is not just the absence of physical imprisonment. True deliverance must flow from every fiber of your being, it is an internal process; it is a freedom that is demonstrated in every aspect of your life and must be envisioned as a palpable reality of who you are. As a result of the aforementioned, genuine deliverance is accompanied by a known strength and resilience that allows you to operate freely in truth, and accept the responsibility that comes with being obedient to the Creator's pre-determined and set plan for your life.

So what is it that He's requiring of you today? It is this; when you move with His leading and function in His truth, you will find yourself in a new dimension of peace. It is in this place of quiet rest that your perspective on life changes. Within this space, your life takes on new meaning, and the willingness to embrace purpose and passion becomes a reality. As a consequence of being emboldened, the expectations that are embedded in His original plan for your life is met with a new found energy and determination that is enveloped with a sense of clarity and precision. It is a radical move which requires that you become brazen enough to sever ties with failed strategies, entities and relationships that keep you tied to your past; ties that are detrimental to your new found perspective on life.

A life of fulfillment requires that a choice be made to say no to the old and yes to the new pathway that is before you. So, why should you risk moving forward on this uncharted path? Because it is your life, you must be resolute and unwavering in the quest to fulfill your purpose and destiny. It is your decision to make, and you can successfully accomplish this task. The choice is yours.

CHAPTER ONE

You were put on this earth to achieve your greatest self, to live out your purpose and to do it courageously.

—Dr Steve Maraboli

The first undeniable truth lies in the need to understand and embrace the realization that for everything, there was, is, and always will be a plan and a purpose for the creation of this universe. Embedded within this reality is the notion of time and seasons that is meant to propel you into having the faith to believe that nothing happens by chance, nor before its time. As you embrace this reality, opportunities are sought to highlight the recognition that the time is now, if ever, to begin the process of engagement with a new conversation about life and its purpose. This life changing conversation is one in which the original blueprint for creation can finally be defined and understood, a blueprint that embodies the predetermined counsel of God. Make no mistake, God is a purposeful God and His creative master plan for mankind was set in motion after careful planning and consideration of what He wanted its beginning and end to look like, and accomplish for His glory. It is at this place, this new reality, that you are expected to grasp the immutability of His counsel, for He counseled with Himself about each and every one of his children. Know that, not one individual's birth was, is, or ever will be a mistake. There is a divine purpose for each life, and errors are not tolerated or accepted in His plan of creation. Hence, it is imperative that you become acutely aware of the truth which allows you to fully comprehend that before the creation of this universe, there was, and still remains a set and determined pathway designed for each individual to follow and complete. Understanding this truth sets in motion the faith to believe that no circumstance or situation can profess the ability to alter what is now understood to be an infallible truth about your life. This absolute truth is not fact. Whereas fact can be altered as a result of erroneous information, truth standing firm, will always endure the test of time. This is why; being in possession of His truth will always set you free, if you are ready and willing to accept its consequences and enduring reality.

Once the above is accepted and internalized, it supersedes any personal, individual or group ideas that were intended to determine by what means a life of purpose and destiny could be achieved. How can this happen; it does so because the Creator and Master Planner concurs with the ultimate Source (Himself) to make a declarative statement intended to ensure that His creation fully understands the premise and intent of His law. For it is written:

> "I alone know the plans I have for you, plans to bring you prosperity and not disaster, plans to bring about the future you hope for" (Jer. 29:11).

Therefore, with this assurance, imperfect man can now totally depend on a trustworthy God, an Omnipotent, Omnipresent and Omniscient God for his future well being. These plans are His, not yours or anyone else's. Strengthened with a heightened belief in His truth, you accept with confidence, the assurance that the Master Creator of the Universe presets your life. Hence, you are now on a set time line with His expectation that all of mankind will adhere too, and produce fruit that has the potential to bring about lasting and life changing results for His Kingdom here on earth.

.

DOCUMENT THE IDEAL PRINCIPLES LEARNT FROM CHAPTER ONE

_____
_____
_____
_____
_____
_____
_____
_____
_____
_____
_____
_____
_____
_____
_____
_____

DR. SHIRLEY PIERRE ROBERTSON

CHAPTER TWO

There are two great days in a person's life – the day we are born and the day we discover why.

—William Barklay

The second undeniable truth lies in the assertion that every human being was born to fulfill a purpose, solve a problem, make a difference, and be a catalyst for change in his or her sphere of influence in the Kingdom of God. In other words, everyone is sent and strategically placed on this earth to fulfill an assignment that is preset to make a significant dent in the kingdom of darkness. That is, to alter and make significant changes, whereby, that which presently exists can become what was originally planned before the beginning of time. It is a tremendous responsibility and undertaking for anyone to conceive of.

Moreover, it can be a painful process to accept and endure. However, it is not an impossible feat to accomplish, for deep within the crucibles of your soul are all the tools and gifts required to complete this earthly assignment. Yet, at some point along the continuum, you must come to terms with the reality that life is more than the sum total of your experiences. As it is often stated, there is more to this life than our eyes can see. Keeping this in mind, it is crucial for you to grasp and hold on to the veracity of this statement; no one is ever sent to fulfill an assignment that they were not first given the ability and talent to accomplish.

And so, having said thus, it is important to note that this gifting and talent does not occur at birth; these attributes were placed in you before the foundation of this world. And so, since creation was purposeful, your arrival here on earth is a testimony to the fact that you are pre-wired and prepared to successfully complete your earthly assignment. Bring to mind the word of God spoken in the Garden of Eden. There, He spoke to Himself and said

"Let us make man in our image, in our likeness, and let them rule over the fish of the sea and the birds of the air, over the livestock, over all the earth, and over all the creatures that move along the ground….God blessed them and said to them, "Be fruitful and increase in number; fill the earth and subdue it. Rule over the fish of the sea and over the birds of the air and over every living creature that moves on the ground" (Gen 1:26-28).

Hence, mankind was designed and built with the tenacity, the resolve to dominate, rule, reign, be fruitful, and increase in the environment in which they were placed. Thus, success is a built in component of our relationship with the Creator, and regardless of the challenges or circumstances you may endure, finishing well remains a defining and enduring factor of His will. Consequently, there is a divine expectation that each individual would trust His word.

DR. SHIRLEY PIERRE ROBERTSON

Therefore, implementing the courage to trust ushers in the self-confidence that is necessary for you to walk by what you believe about your Creator, and not by what the limitations of your sight allows you to see and believe.

DOCUMENT THE IDEAL PRINCIPLES LEARNT FROM CHAPTER TWO

_____
_____
_____
_____
_____
_____
_____
_____
_____
_____
_____
_____
_____
_____

DR. SHIRLEY PIERRE ROBERTSON

CHAPTER THREE

If you can't figure out your purpose, figure out your passion. For your passion will lead you directly to your purpose.

—Evan Carmichael

The third undeniable truth lies in the need to become intimately connected to your passion. Passion is that which stirs within you a desire that comes from the heart, it is an inner longing to do and go after something. It is a mindset which gives you free rein to go above and beyond all of the normal expectations for your life; it transcends the notion of "what if" and motivates you to satisfy the longing, the yearning to become more than anything your current situation dictates. It is this momentum, this drive that is meant to unlock for you an urgent need to get with His agenda in order to pursue your purpose for being. Like the

Apostle Paul, it was through a Damascus Road conversion experience that his primary attributes; his zeal to persecute the church was shattered. This unsubstantiated zeal to destroy, was transformed by that which is unapologetically immeasurable in His power to set a changed course for a new way of living and being.

We therefore take note of the truth as laid out in Acts Chapter 9 where Paul transitioned to a different purpose with his life. His zeal to persecute and destroy his fellow man was re-channeled, and thus became his passion to know and serve his Maker and Creator. So, in Romans 1:14-15 Paul demonstrates this new found reality with the following statement:

"I am a debtor to the Greeks and the Barbarians; both to the wise, and the unwise. So, as much as in me is, I am ready to preach the gospel to you that are in Rome also" (NKJV).

Here, Paul makes note of the fact that he is obligated to do the will of God, and to preach the good news of the gospel to the lost. However, this obligation is entwined, closely liked to his passion, and he was committed to seeing it through to the end. Thus, from his life, you are admonished to learn how passion becomes the fuel that ignites and drives your decision to stand alone if need be in the face of opposition, lack of support and criticism, in order to fulfill God's vision and divine purpose for your life.

Once this new move becomes a reality, it is imperative that you stay in your lane, excel and dominate in your sphere of influence. Put an unyielding trust in your Creator who gave you the confidence to move forward and work your lane with the peace "which transcends all understanding…." (Phil 4:7) knowing that you are an original, no one has your brand, and that no one can achieve that which you were designed and sent to accomplish. It is imperative that you understand and internalize the reality that you can never be copied for the set reason that you are a designer's original; you are one of a kind. Every designer, who prides his work on the ability to be an original in his creative sphere boast about this, and therefore has the potential to command exorbitant fees. These prices are based on the premise that the wearer of his work must have no fear of walking the red carpet, only to realize that their prized possession was duplicated. Far above the intent of an earthly creator, lies the Master Creator of the Universe. Your Creator, your God, His creation and His eternal plans for each and everyone remains unabashedly intact. Therefore, be assured that you were prewired and sent to accomplish a task, and bring about change that only your calling and anointing can confront and influence.

Again, there is only one you, so fear not. This means that, of the more than seven billion human beings who occupy this planet called earth, not one individual can attest to having your fingerprint, your unique characteristics. Furthermore, there is absolutely nothing to fear from the challenges posed by anyone. Allow your vision for "being" to keep you focused and never become frustrated or anxious when others appear to be excelling ahead of you. Rather, use these feelings to challenge and catapult yourself to the next level, and learn to turn your negative energy into the positive fuel that is required for success.

Remember that there are many trailblazers who have gone ahead of you. More often than not, they have paid the price to open doors that were heretofore closed. But your unique approach, fresh and unexplored ideas, an embolden spirit to never give up and never give in, will afford you the opportunity to stand above the crowd and excel. Once your quest to succeed is understood, it paves the way for the development of a quiet and confident determination to do your pre-assigned work, as you align yourself with others of like passion and purpose. Furthermore, when you correctly position yourself and network with like-minded individuals and groups, you are now capable of achieving much more than you ever could have accomplished on your own.

It has often been said that all it takes for mutual success to occur is for one iron to sharpen another. The positive aspect of this exchange or trade off allows fusion to occur, thus making room for the intended and big picture of the Creator to emerge. Fusion here is meant to denote that each person is ready and willing to operate and excel in their set position of influence and excellence, without becoming intimidated by the skill set and talent of others. It is here, where the personal and self centered ambitions of a few, takes a back seat for the good of the whole. Within this scenario, opportunities to learn and grow present themselves as a definite advantage to those who are willing to demonstrate the attributes that are required to be a team player.

Always remember this; you will aspire and achieve to your maximum potential when you understand and accept that you were given enough talent to meet the expectations of the Creator. There is no need to fight this process, because it requires as much energy and effort for the one-talent person to maximize his potential as it does for the five-talent person to capitalize and grow that, which was entrusted to him. Thus, within this atmosphere, failure is never embraced as an option to quit or give up. This environment concurs with the premise that it matters not how many times you have failed or your efforts have gone belly up; the main imperative here is that you continue to fail your way to success. Keep in mind that each person is accountable for that which they are entrusted with, because accountability is an integral aspect of stewardship.

Everyone must give an account for either accomplishing or abandoning his or her reason for being. For this cause, you must be ever faithful to the successful completion of your God ordained purpose.

DR. SHIRLEY PIERRE ROBERTSON

DOCUMENT THE IDEAL PRINCIPLES LEARNT FROM CHAPTER THREE

_____
_____
_____
_____
_____
_____
_____
_____
_____
_____
_____
_____
_____
_____
_____

YOUR PASSION YOUR PURPOSE

CHAPTER FOUR

If you correct your mind, the rest will fall into place.

—Lso-Tzu

The fourth undeniable truth lies in the urgent need to be receptive of and internalize that a transformed mind ushers in a change of attitude, the positive result of which is a change in behavior. Having ascertained the truth regarding the will of the Creator regarding who you are, and whose you are, it is now time to immerse yourself in this undisputable declaration that was made over your life:

"For I know the plans I have for you," declares the LORD, plans to prosper you and not to harm you, plans to give you hope and a future (Jer. 29:11).

Least you forget, this thought further admonishes you to keep true to your promise, while remembering that neither friend or foe, principalities or power can alter the outcome for your life if you:

"Do not conform any longer to the pattern of this world, but be transformed by the renewing of your mind. Then you will be able to test and approve what God's will is—His good, pleasing, and perfect will" (Romans 12:2).

The willingness to accept that a transformed mind has the propensity to shift and replace "can't do" thinking with "can do" is the catalyst that is required for change to occur. As the way becomes clear for movement to take place, you are now open, receptive, and ready to do the work that is required to replace old ways with a series of positive life changing strategies. However, this new mindset must be inculcated, nurtured and re-enforced with the willingness to examine old behaviors, because excuses will not prevail in this arena.

Remember the children of Israel? After crying out to their God and experiencing His awesome power, and their eventual deliverance out of Egypt when faced with challenges, their minds quickly returned back to Egypt. Physically they were no longer in bondage, but their minds were yet to embrace the truth of total freedom and what that entailed, so:

> They said to Moses "was it because there were no graves in Egypt that you brought us to the desert to die? What have you done to us by bringing us out of Egypt? Didn't we say to you in Egypt, "Leave us alone; let us serve the Egyptians? It would have been better for us to serve the Egyptians than to die in the desert!" Moses answered the people, "Do not be afraid. Stand firm and you will see the deliverance the LORD will bring you today. The Egyptians you see today you will never see again. The LORD will fight for you; you need only to be still." Then the LORD said to Moses " Why are you crying out to me? Tell the Israelites to move on"
> (Exodus 14:11-15).

Indeed it is time to move on, it is time to rid yourself of the old mentality of always wanting to return your mind to its familiar place of abode, where fear and anxiety reside. Why? Because whom the Son has set free is free indeed, and where true freedom lays it encompasses the totality of your being. In this place called "there" oppression in any shape or form cannot survive. Yet, in spite of this reality, mental freedom is a choice. It is the ability, the power to make a conscious decision to exercise your free will to choose between life and death, success or failure, the path least travelled, or the one in which there is an over abundance of casualties. Think carefully on this, for the choice to move forward and upward is yours to make and implement.

Notwithstanding is the fact that you should not bemoan your past. Utilize the lessons learnt from these experiences to develop positive bridge building strategies that would move you away from your familiar mountain, and into your promised land.

Once your purpose for being is understood and embraced, it will energize you. Your vision becomes clear, your confidence level soars, and your motivation to overcome obstacles that are detrimental to your success are taken to a new dimension in life. Truly, this is what change looks like, and it demonstrates the reality of a transformed mind that is determined to accept the truth as promised by the Creator. He has the perfect plan for your life; one in which hope and a bright future is assured. Mortal man may verbalize this thought to you, but he does not possess the capacity or the capability to bring his promises to fruition.

DR. SHIRLEY PIERRE ROBERTSON

DOCUMENT THE IDEAL PRINCIPLES LEARNT FROM CHAPTER FOUR

_____
_____
_____
_____
_____
_____
_____
_____
_____
_____
_____
_____
_____
_____

YOUR PASSION YOUR PURPOSE

CHAPTER FIVE

Choose not to settle. Pursue your God-given goals, knowing it's never too late to accomplish everything God has placed in your heart.

—Baby G Swag

The fifth undeniable truth acknowledges that age is not a deterrent to the pursuit of purpose. It is never too late to begin the process of accomplishing that which you were sent here to do. Though the gifts within you may be lying dormant, as long as you are alive they will never die. Regardless of the turns you make on this journey called life, be they positive or negative, purpose remains constant because of the immutability of God's promises. Thus, the need to be and become is ever present and it is meant to move you from where you are to where you ought to be.

This unsettling feeling; this emptiness, restlessness, not being satisfied with life, often times leads to the manifestation of depression and other mental health related issues. Many resort to unproductive and destructive behavior patterns, in an effort to quell the inner turmoil and pain that they are experiencing. The negative effects of this stressful experience can be debilitating if answers to the who, the why, and the where of your existence is not made readily available to you.

Once it is understood that you are more than the sum total of life's challenges; that regardless of how painful those experiences were for you, your purpose and credibility will emerge from your life story. Having gained insight into God's process for your life, the knowledge and wisdom obtained gives you the wherewithal to become clear-sighted and encouraged. Consequently, a healthy determination begins to glean positive nuggets that are ripe with the strength required to move you in an upright and forward direction. Always remember that you are not on your own, neither are you your own. Your Creator, who knew every twist and turn that you would encounter on this journey called life, has a word for you:

> "Behold, I am the Lord, the God of all flesh: is there anything too hard for me" (Jer. 32; 27).

In other words, He's saying to you; look here, whatever the problem is, whatever the issues are, I am more than enough, more than able to help you, deliver you, and set you free from your whatsoever. I will do this, so that you can get on with the task that is set before you; that which you've always wanted to do, that which lights a fire of passion within you. I am here to support you in the achievement of your purpose, and I do not require your assistance with this venture. My aim and intent is that you do not leave this world having not implemented and fulfilled the plans that were made for your life. Therefore, I am here to work with you.

As you ponder on this perspective with a renewed mind, consider that the Bible left us with a legacy of testimonials regarding those trailblazers who willingly, or otherwise, were called to fulfill their purpose. Thus, the answer to the question: why was I born, can be garnered from the life of Abraham. Recall how he was called to move from his familiar place with this covenantal promise:

> "…Leave your country, your people and your father's household and go to the land I will show you. I will make you into a great nation and I will bless you; I will make your name great, and you will be a blessing. I will bless those who bless you, and whoever curses you I will curse; and all peoples on earth will be blessed through you" (Gen. 12: 1-3).

He was seventy-five years of age and childless, but Abraham believed the Word of his Maker and Creator. Therefore, we have absolutely no reason to give our Creator any more excuses. After all; whose report would you believe, if not the one coming for the mouth of Him who knows all things and sees all things, The Alpha and Omega, the Beginning and the End. Abraham's life experiences had prepared him for this new chapter, this life-changing directive, and this faith-embracing journey of a lifetime. This was a game changer, for without any evidence of things that were not seen he chose to trust the Word of God.

Suffice it to say that within the providential actions of the Master, is the built in expectation of a confidence that exudes with understanding and trust. In other words, it is an empowering manifestation of truth, which depicts and relays the immutability of His knowing what is best for His children. In view of this knowledge and understanding, what is released is the wisdom to accept and believe that the good, the bad and the ugly of our experiences indeed:

"….work together for good…to them who are the called according to His purpose" (Romans 8:28)

Moses on the other hand was eighty-nine years of age when the burning bush caught his attention. When that which was settled in eternity met with its designated time here on earth, Moses was called by his Maker and Creator to fulfill his purpose for being with the following statement:

"And now the cry of the Israelites have reached me, and I have seen the way that the Egyptians are oppressing them. So now, go, I am sending you to Pharaoh to bring my people the Israelites out of Egypt" (Exodus 3: 9-10)

But, unlike Abraham, Moses began to make excuses about his ability to follow through with the clarion call to emerge as the Creator's mouthpiece and tool, in the deliverance of the children of Israel from Egyptian bondage. Instead of displaying total acceptance of his calling, unbelief and fear of the unknown took precedence over his passion to see his people go free. Thus, his immediate response was this:

"....Who am I that I should go to Pharaoh and bring the Israelites out of Egypt" (Exodus 3:11).

Age, a speech impediment, and being raised separately from the nation he was mandated to lead, could not deter the manifestation of that which was pre determined in the heavenly to become a reality here on earth. And, as was previously stated, when eternity meets time, a cataclysmic reaction takes place and everything therefore falls into place as it is meant to be. Nothing and no one can alter this process, and nothing happens by chance. However, Moses response was not surprising to his Creator, thus Aaron was pre assigned in eternity to be his mouthpiece. Problem fixed! The Master of the Universe did not stop to scratch His head and ponder His next move. He already knew that Moses arrived on this earth equipped with the necessary talent and skill set to become a leader, one who was chosen and destined to leave an indelible mark in the annals of biblical history. After all, why was he saved from Pharaoh's quest to reduce the ever-populating numbers of Israelites, from drowning in the River Nile, or from being caught after he murdered the Egyptian slave master for smiting a Hebrew slave. Moses divine purpose had to be fulfilled in-spite of his past experiences, and his proclivities. These occurrences had absolutely no power to alter the original plan of his Creator. Moses was a wanted man who was born on time, for such a time as his Creator chose.

The same goes for you and I. Our past has no power to determine or dictate our future. However, the Master Creator of the universe allows nothing to go to waste in His Kingdom, since everything is used as required fuel to catapult you into your true calling. As such, do not despise your past, but embrace its potential to be the stepping-stone from which you can now launch out into your purpose.

I have learnt, as I continue to move forward on my journey that I cannot be everybody, but I can be somebody who is determined to walk in the calling in which He endowed me to be. I am confident enough through His grace to honor others for their gifts and calling but I am not, cannot, and never will be anyone other than who He created me to be and become. Moving in this knowledge and understanding, I can deploy my potential to craft and master a pathway of transforming persuasiveness that is incomparable and determined, to make a significant impact in the lives of others. So I strive to leave a legacy, a positive contribution, even if it is only this: that it is never too late to fulfill your dreams. At 62 years of age I answered the call of my Creator to begin my doctoral studies. And in the midst of my obedience to the will of God, my husband suffered a stroke and I became his fulltime caregiver. However, at age 67, I graduated with a Doctoral Degree (Ed.D) in Education with a dual specialization in Organizational Leadership and Human

Services Administration; a 4.0 grade point average (the highest for that program), the Grandmother of my class, and one of only a few at that time to complete the program. Yes! It took courage, faith, and tenacity to honor my ancestors, my parents and myself. But most importantly, the calling to be who He created me to be took precedence over my personal feelings. Was it difficult? Sure it was. There were periods during which the pain was so intense with caring for my husband that I could not see the forest for the trees. Many sleepless nights were spent crying in the midst of caring. My needs took a back seat to his needs and the commitment that was made during our marriage ceremony. Are you familiar with the wording of these vows: for better or for worse, in sickness and in health, for richer or for poorer, till death do us part? Never ever agree to that which you are not prepared to follow through with. Furthermore, there were vows I made to my Abba, my Daddy, my God that I would surrender my life to Him totally, and was willing and available to be used by Him in whatever capacity He chose for my life. Oh yes, He accepted and took this commitment very serious. What kept me going through some of my darkest periods were scriptural passages like the following:

> For His anger last only a moment, but His favor last a lifetime; weeping may remain for a night, but rejoicing comes in the morning (Psalm 30:5).

> And the God of all grace, who called you to His eternal glory in Christ, after you have suffered a little while, will Himself restore you and make you strong, firm, and steadfast
> (1 Peter 5:10).

> God is not unjust: He will not forget your work and the love you have shown Him as you have helped His people and continue to help them (Hebrews 6:10).

You see, it is impossible to make known the fact that you are willing and capable of caring for others without first demonstrating this charitable quality at home. In order to prove this, my Abba in His wisdom allowed circumstance to occur in order to showcase the resilience and brilliance, which He in eternity had placed within me for His appropriate time. This experience eventually changed my life for the better, to the point where I can now declare that it has worked in my favor. I am now fully cognizant of His truth, which declares the following:

> And we know that all things work together for good to those who love God, to those who are called according to His purpose (romans 8:28).

As a result of this experience and many others, my purpose has been sharpened. I understand my calling, and my focus is on point. I know who I am in His kingdom; this is my future.

Be that as it may, realizing that your purpose is your future necessitates the ability to grasp in essence, that a pre-requisite to its attainment is patience. However, do not ask for patience to pursue purpose unless you are prepared to endure and successfully pass the test that is assigned to the attainment of this great attribute. Yes indeed, patience is needed to press forward in the face of some of life's most debilitating challenges.

Learn to give thanks for your journey as you may very well discover through the process, the Why of your birth, and the problems that were pre-assigned for your attention and resolution. Be assertive, stand up and declare this Why as you prepare to unleash the solutions that are already within you. Acknowledge that no one else can solve the problem that was assigned to you as competently and effectively as you can. Embrace the truth that out of almost five hundred million sperms, that God ordained just one to impregnated the egg that would be you. What a feat! Therefore, take others breath away as you defy the odds that were taken against your ability to succeed at being the champion for a pre-assigned cause. Reach deep within, for that which is in you is priceless; it cannot be bought with silver or gold. Stand up and stand out. Never be afraid to tell your story because it could be the deciding factor between hope and continued despair for another human being. As you ponder on your life and where you are at this juncture, remember this:

> All you need is the plan, the roadmap, and the courage to press on to your destination
> (Earl Nightingale)

I encourage you therefore to have the faith like Abraham, to believe that your God and Creator is not a man who tells lies, neither is there any logical argument that can modify the potential of His supreme power to make the impossible become possible for you. Why shouldn't you believe in who you are, whose you are, and in your power to be and become who you are. Dare to believe that your future is looking good; but it's up to you to embrace this truth. Pursue your purpose in order to leave a legacy. Deprive the grave of its potential to declare you as one who failed, because of unbelief and the absence of faith to maximize your gifts and calling. Suffice it to say that my declarative statement to you and others is this: that neither age or adverse experiences have the capability nor capacity to alter His immutable plan for your life and purpose in the Kingdom of God. Therefore, allow the resilience and brilliance that is within you to be the propelling force that thrust you into becoming your authentic self. In other words, may the real you please stand up and occupy your preordained position in the Kingdom of God. Pursue your purpose with passion.

DR. SHIRLEY PIERRE ROBERTSON

DOCUMENT THE IDEAL PRINCIPLES LEARNT FROM CHAPTER FIVE

_____
_____
_____
_____
_____
_____
_____
_____
_____
_____
_____
_____
_____
_____
_____
_____

YOUR PASSION YOUR PURPOSE

ABOUT THE AUTHOR

Dr Shirley Pierre Robertson is an Ordained Minister, Mental Health Professional, Christian Life Purpose Coach, Transformational Speaker, Retired Adjunct Professor, Entrepreneur and Retreat Facilitator. She is the Founder and CEO of Designed To Shine International, Inc. an all-embracing and wide ranging initiative, whose intent and overriding purpose is to restore back to individuals, families, and communities their original purpose for being in the Kingdom of God.

As a native of Trinidad and Tobago, Dr Pierre Robertson received her formal training as a nurse in London, England and Toronto Canada, a Diploma in Christian Life Coaching with a specialization in Stress Management from Light University Virginia, and is a Certified Professional Wellness Trainer from The Professional Women Network, Louisville, KY. She also studied for and obtained a BA in Psychology from York University, Toronto Canada,

DR. SHIRLEY PIERRE ROBERTSON

a B.Sc. in Nursing from the University of Alberta, Canada, an MS in Psychiatric/Mental Health Nursing and Education from the University of Maryland, Baltimore, MD, and a Doctorate in Education (Ed.D) with a dual specialization in Organizational Leadership and Human Services Administration from Nova Southeastern University, Ft Lauderdale, Florida.

www.ingramcontent.com/pod-product-compliance
Lightning Source LLC
LaVergne TN
LVHW051202080426
835508LV00021B/2769